Frank Sinatra Songbook

Acknowledgement

A special thanks to Frank Military.
Without his unswerving dedication, this
book would not have been possible.

© 1989 WARNER BROS. PUBLICATIONS INC.

All the Best,
Frank Sinatra

FRANK SINATRA

Frank Sinatra has long been acclaimed as the world's leading performer of popular music; the artist who set the mold for all others to fill. He is, of course, more than a singer – Frank Sinatra is also an actor, recording artist, cabaret and concert star, radio and television personality and, on occasion, a producer, director and conductor. His career, which includes acting roles in more than 50 films, some of which he produced and directed, is studded with accolades: Oscars, Grammys, Emmys, the prestigious Peabody Award. A dedicated humanitarian, he has received numerous honors and awards in appreciation of his charitable endeavors.

A performer for nearly five decades, Mr. Sinatra shows no signs of slowing down. His life in recent years has been marked by prodigious activity in films, concerts, recordings and cabaret appearances.

He returned to the screen in "The First Deadly Sin," released the blockbuster album, the three-record "Trilogy;" "She Shot Me Down" and "L.A. Is My Lady." He has performed at Rio de Janeiro's Maracana Soccer Stadium before the largest audience (175,000) ever to attend a concert by a soloist (the event is recorded in the Guinness Book of World Records) and served as producer and director of entertainment for President Reagan's Inaugural Galas in 1981 and 1985.

Among his recent honors are the Presidential Medal of Freedom, the nation's highest award, which he received at a White House ceremony; an honorary Doctorate of Engineering from the Stevens Institute of Technology in Hoboken, New Jersey; and Austria's Medal of Honor for Science and Art, First Class, which he received following his benefit in Vienna to aid handicapped children.

Mr. Sinatra also appeared in several successive annual engagements at Carnegie Hall, each surpassing the previous year in critical acclaim and box office success. Indeed, he has established several box office records at that fabled landmark.

During his illustrious career, Mr. Sinatra acquired such famous nicknames as The Chairman of the Board, The Voice, The Greatest Roman of Them All and, of course, as virtually the entire world knows him, Ol' Blue Eyes. The whole world also knows that he was born Francis Albert Sinatra in Hoboken, N.J. As a youngster, he had visions of a sportswriting career and worked briefly as a copy boy for a local newspaper. However, that ambition was short-lived once Frank Sinatra heard the unique music-styles of Billie Holiday and Bing Crosby. He decided to pursue a singing career himself and started with a local group called the Hoboken Four. It didn't last very long, and when the quartet broke up, the young singer took the solo route and toured the vaudeville circuit. Eventually he landed a job as a singing MC at the Rustic Cabin, a roadhouse in Englewood, N.J. His talent attracted Harry James, who hired him as a band vocalist. It was 1939, the heyday of the big bands and Frank Sinatra was on his way. A year later he joined Tommy Dorsey and began recording with the band's vocal group, the fondly remembered Pied Pipers.

"The Voice" later struck out on his own and appeared on radio's "Your Hit Parade" and his own show, "Songs By Sinatra." Then, in late 1942, he appeared at the old Paramount Theatre on Times Square. The headliner on the bill was Benny Goodman and when the bandleader introduced Mr. Sinatra, the audience erupted and cheered itself hoarse. There was dancing in the aisles, whistling, whooping and shrieking and it was the beginning of a long love affair between the singer and his fans. It was one of the most spectacular events in show business history and Frank Sinatra's career went soaring.

The next year, he made his movie debut and went on to appear in such notable films as "Anchors Aweigh," "On The Town," "The Man With The Golden Arm," "Pal Joey," "The Manchurian Candidate" and, "From Here To Eternity," the motion picture which brought him an Academy Award as Best Supporting Actor. He also received a special Oscar for "The House I Live In," the documentary that made an eloquent plea for an end to prejudice of all kinds. During the 1960's, Mr. Sinatra established his own recording company, Reprise Records, and released a number of well-remembered hit albums. During those years, he also starred in several award-winning one-man TV specials.

In 1978, he went to Israel for the dedication of the Frank Sinatra International Student Centre at the Mount Scopus campus of the Hebrew University (another building in Israel named for him is the Frank Sinatra Youth Centre in Nazareth). The following year he returned to the Middle East, performing a benefit concert in Egypt at the request of Madam Sadat for her favorite charity.

Mr. Sinatra has kept, as is customary, a busy schedule: tours to the U.S. and Europe; cabaret engagements; his role as Abbot of the New York Friars Club; a special appearance in Chicago at the city's annual ChicagoFest; a concert at the opening of a new 5,000-seat amphitheatre in Altos de Chavon in the Dominican Republic that was taped by Paramount Video and later broadcast on pay-TV systems around the country and induction into the National Broadcasters Hall of Fame.

He recently recorded "To Love A Child," the theme song of the Foster Grandparents Program, a favorite project of Nancy Reagan and the title of a book she has written. Proceeds from the record, which is dedicated to the First Lady, go to the program.

Frank Sinatra has received numerous honors of distinction. Variety Clubs International, the show business charity, saluted him for his achievements as an entertainer and a humanitarian. The event, which was attended by scores of Sinatra's celebrity friends, was a CBS-TV special. As a tribute to him, the Sinatra Family Children's Unit for the Chronically Ill was established at the Seattle Children's Orthopedic Hospital and Medical Center. Mr. Sinatra was one of the five distinguished honorees – the others were Jimmy Stewart, Eliz Kazan , Virgil Thompson and Katherine Dunham – of the 1983 Kennedy Center Honors.

Mr. Sinatra's world-wide travels in recent years have taken him to Vienna, London (at the Royal Albert Hall, where he is a perennial favorite), Paris (at the famed Moulin Rouge), Tokyo, Italy, South America and Honolulu, where he performed for the first time in 30 years and where he had filmed "From Here To Eternity" and "None But The Brave."

Despite a heavy schedule of professional commitments, Frank Sinatra somehow manages to find the time to lend his talents to humanitarian causes, performing benefit concerts in the U.S. and overseas and participating in numerous fund-raising drives. Among the organizations which have benefited from his activities are the Red Cross, Palm Springs' Desert Hospital, Variety Clubs International, the New York PAL, Cabrini Medical Center, the World Mercy Fund, the University of Nevada at Las Vegas, and the National Multiple Sclerosis Society. A particular favorite is the Barbara Sinatra Children's Center at Eisenhower Medical Center in Palm Springs, Ca. His wife, Barbara, is the driving force behind the two-year old facility which treats victims of sexual and physical abuse.

His upcoming activities include recording an all-digital album for CD release, produced by his son, Frank Sinatra, Jr. for Reprise Records. It will include songs never before recorded by Sinatra, Sr.

CONTENTS

Special photo section pages 169-176

One of Frank's most popular closers, this Kander and Ebb song was first introduced by Liza Minnelli in the film of the same name. Frank's recording appears on "Trilogy."

Theme From New York, New York

Words by
FRED EBB

Music by
JOHN KANDER

A showstopper at concerts, this song was originally written by three French songwriters. Paul Anka penned the English lyrics, and Don Costa made the arrangement. A live recording made during Frank's 1974 United States tour was released on "Sinatra - The Main Event."

My Way

Original French Lyrics by
GILLES THIBAULT
English Lyrics by
PAUL ANKA

Music by
CLAUDE FRANCOIS
and JACQUES REVAUX

Written for "The Joker Is Wild," Frank portrayed comedian Joe E. Lewis and gave another outstanding performance. The song was recorded twice: for Capitol (August 13, 1957), and for Reprise (April 29, 1963). Both featured the classic Nelson Riddle score.

All The Way

Words by
SAMMY CAHN

Music by
JAMES VAN HEUSEN

Ira Gershwin wrote new lyrics for Frank to record for the "No One Cares" album. Gordon Jenkins arranged and conducted the recording on March 26, 1959.

I Can't Get Started

Words by
IRA GERSHWIN

Music by
VERNON DUKE

I'm a glum one, it's ex-plain-a-ble: I met some one un-at-tain-a-ble;

Life's a bore, The world is my oy-ster no more.

I'm a glum one; it's explainable:
I met someone unattainable.
    Life's a bore,
The world is my oyster no more.
All the papers, where I led the news
With my capers, now will spread the news:
    "Superman
Turns out to be Flash In The Pan!"

First Refrain

I've flown through outer space in a plane;
I've made the moon my secret domain.
   The Russians I've outsmarted—
   But can't get started with you.

All the Olympic medals I've won
Prove my physique is second to none;
   My heart is big and roomy
   What good's it do me with you.

    When first we met—
How you elated me!
    Pet!
You devastated me!
    Yet—
Now you've deflated me
Till you're my Waterloo.

In Cincinnati or in Rangoon
I smile and gals go into a swoon;
   But you've got me down-hearted
   'Cause I can't get started with you.

Second Refrain

I'm written up in *Fortune* and *Time*;
The biggest and the latest news, I'm.
   For me they strike the band up . . . .
   I'm just a stand-up with you.

* D'you know the Texas taxes I pay?
(I gush a million barrels a day).
   Each house I own's a show place
   But I get no place with you.

    Oh, tell me why
Am I no kick to you—
    I,
Who'd always stick to you.
    Fly—
Through thick and thin to you?
Tell me why I'm taboo!

I offer you a man among mice—
(I could have been the President twice!)
   With queens I've a la carted—
   But I can't get started with you.

*NOTE FROM THE AUTHOR:
  An excellent substitute for this stanza:

I'm welcomed anywhere I may be;
Why, Greta Garbo's had me to tea.
   The Ira Gershwins I visit,
   But, say, what *is* it with you?

Frank's version of this Jerome Kern classic is a highlight of the film "Till The Clouds Roll By." His Columbia record, with Axel Stordahl at the podium, was waxed on December 3, 1944.

Ol' Man River

Words by
OSCAR HAMMERSTEIN

Music by
JEROME KERN

A showstopper at concerts, Frank recorded this Frank Foster score for the "L.A. Is My Lady" album.

Mack The Knife
From "The Threepenny Opera"

English Words by
MARC BLITZSTEIN
(Original German Words
by BERT BRECHT)

Music by
KURT WEILL

2. On the sidewalk, one Sunday morning,
lies a body oozing life.
Someone's sneakin' 'round the corner.
Could that someone, perchance, be Mack the Knife?

From a tugboat, by the river goin' slow,
a cement bag's droppin' down.
And the cement's just, just for the weight, dear,
I bet you Mackie's, yeah, he's back in town.

3. My man Louie Miller, he split the scene, babe,
after drawin' out all the bread in his stash.
And Macheath spends just like a "pimp" now;
did our boy do, did he do somethin' rash?

Oh, Satchmo—Louis Armstrong, Bobby Darin,
they did this song nice, and Lady Ella, too.
They all sang it, sang it with such feeling
that Ol' Blue Eyes can't add nothin' new.

4. But with Quincy's big band right behind me,
swingin' hard, Jack, I know I can't lose.
When I tell you how Mack the Knife paid,
it's an offer you can't refuse.

We got George Benson, Newman, Foster,
Yeah, we got the Brecker Brothers,
and Hamp' bringin' up the rear.
All those bad cats, and more, are in this band now
with the greatest sounds you've ever gonna hear.

D.S. Ah, Sukey Tawdry, old Jenny Diver, Polly Peachum,
and Miss Lucy Brown.
Oh, the line forms on the right, dear,
now that Mackie's, yes, Mackie's,
I said Mackie's, that bad man Mackie,
my man, Mackie, you better know that
Mackie's back in town.

Frank has commissioned scores of this song from George Siravo (recorded November 5, 1953 for Capitol) and by Neal Hefti (recorded April 10, 1962 for Reprise).

They Can't Take That Away From Me

Music and Lyrics by
GEORGE GERSHWIN and IRA GERSHWIN

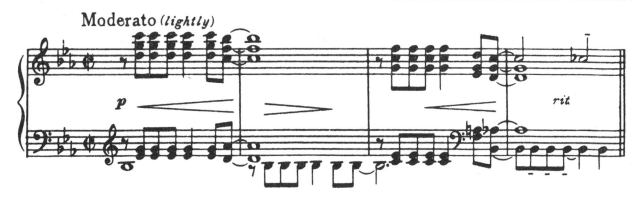

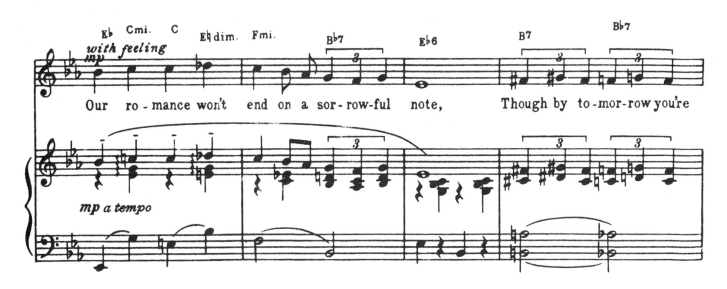

"Ol' Blue Eyes" came back in 1973 to record a memorable album of brand new songs. Joe Raposo wrote this song especially for Frank, and Gordon Jenkins arranged and conducted it on June 21, 1973.

Winners

Theme From Maurie

Words and Music by
JOE RAPOSO

One of Frank's most beautiful ballad sides, it was arranged by Axel Stordahl for the Columbia session of August 22, 1945. Stordahl was one of the composers of the song.

Day By Day

Words and Music by
SAMMY CAHN, AXEL STORDAHL
and PAUL WESTON

One of Frank's earliest recordings with the Tommy Dorsey Orchestra, recorded on March 29, 1940.

Fools Rush In
(Where Angels Fear To Tread)

Words by
JOHNNY MERCER

Music by
RUBE BLOOM

Another Nelson Riddle score that remains in Frank's concert repertoire, it was first taped for Capitol on November 26, 1956 ("Pal Joey" soundtrack).

The Lady Is A Tramp

From "Babes In Arms"

Words by
LORENZ HART

Music by
RICHARD RODGERS

Frank recorded this song three times. The first, for Columbia, was recorded on July 10, 1949. The third version was arranged and conducted by Nelson Riddle on August 23, 1960 and it was a "Swingin' Session."

It All Depends On You

Words and Music by
B.G. DESYLVA, LEW BROWN
and RAY HENDERSON

Lov-ers de-pend on moon-light For a love af-fair.
Is-n't it sweet to know, dear, You can help me on?

Ba-bies de-pend on moth-ers For their ten-der care.
Would-n't it hurt to know, dear, All my hopes were gone?

Axel Stordahl arranged and conducted this song from the show "Oh Kay" on July 30, 1945.

Someone To Watch Over Me

Music and Lyrics by
GEORGE GERSHWIN and IRA GERSHWIN

Another classic Sinatra-Riddle side from "Only The Lonely," which many fans consider to be Frank's finest ballad album.

Blues In The Night

(My Mama Done Tol' Me)

Words by
JOHNNY MERCER

Music by
HAROLD ARLEN

Frank recorded this with Nelson Riddle on November 6, 1953. He later had Neal Hefti write a score for Sinatra's
album with the Count Basie band. This arrangement was prominently featured in "The Main Event" at Madison
Square Garden.

I Get A Kick Out Of You

Words and Music by
COLE PORTER

Already a standard, this Joe Raposo song was composed especially for "Ol' Blue Eyes Is Back." Recorded on June 4, 1973, it was arranged and conducted by Frank's old friend, Gordon Jenkins.

You Will Be My Music

Words and Music by
JOE RAPOSO

I'll be lost and try - ing_____ for songs I'll nev - er sing,

want - ing you

is ev - 'ry - thing.

D.S. 𝄋 al Coda 𝄌

Coda

wrong.

I can't wait an - y long -

rit.

er for my song._____

For the album "Sinatra's Swinging Session!", Frank and Nelson Riddle taped this on August 31, 1960.

September In The Rain

Words by
AL DUBIN

Music by
HARRY WARREN

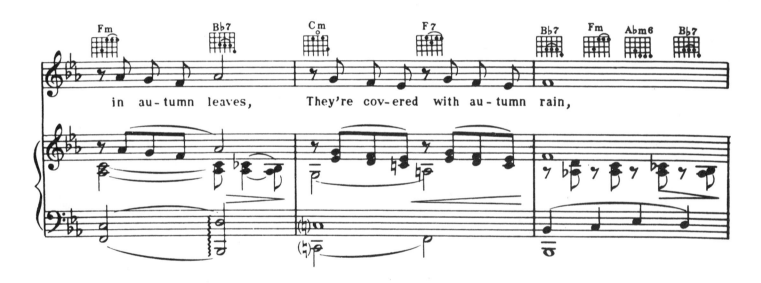

My day dreams lie bur-ied in au-tumn leaves, They're cov-ered with au-tumn rain,

The time is sweet Sep-tem-ber, The place, a shad-y lane,

Frank's recording appears on "That's Life," arranged by Ernie Freeman. They recorded it on November 17, 1966.

What Now My Love

(Original French Version "Et Maintenant")

Original French Lyric by
P. DELANOE
English Lyric by
CARL SIGMAN

Music by
G. BÉCAUD

From the film "Dames," Frank and Axel Stordahl made this recording on August 27, 1945.

I Only Have Eyes For You

Words by
AL DUBIN

Music by
HARRY WARREN

REFRAIN

Nelson Riddle arranged this Cole Porter song for Frank for the January 12, 1956 Capitol session. That version, released on "Songs for Swingin' Lovers," became an immediate classic. It has become one of Frank's most requested songs at concerts.

I've Got You Under My Skin

Words and Music by
COLE PORTER

Frank and Axel Stordahl recorded this great Rodgers and Hart standard for Columbia on August 8, 1946.

Falling In Love With Love

(From "The Boys From Syracuse")

Words by
LORENZ HART

Music by
RICHARD RODGERS

I weave with bright-ly col-ored strings To keep my mind off oth-er things; So, la-dies, let your fin-gers

With the ending of the AFM recording ban, Frank could record with a full orchestra again. Axel Stordahl arranged this swinging Cahn-Styne gem for the Columbia session of November 14, 1944.

Saturday Night
(Is The Loneliest Night Of The Week)

Words by
SAMMY CAHN

Music by
JULE STYNE

One of George Siravo's arrangements, this was cut on April 24, 1950. Sinatra later recorded it with a Nelson Riddle score on August 31, 1960 for "Sinatra's Swinging Session!".

It's Only A Paper Moon

Words by
BILLY ROSE and E.Y. HARBURG

Music by
HAROLD ARLEN

Cole Porter wrote this wartime hit. Frank included it in "A Swingin' Affair" with an arrangement by Nelson Riddle.

You'd Be So Nice To Come Home To

(From "Something To Shout About")

Words and Music by
COLE PORTER

A highlight of "Trilogy - The Present," featuring a stunning Don Costa setting.

Summer Me, Winter Me

(Theme From Picasso Summer)

Words by
MARILYN and ALAN BERGMAN

Music by
MICHEL LEGRAND

The Capitol years yielded two versions of this holiday perennial. The first was only issued as a single (recorded August 23, 1954), the second was recorded for "A Jolly Christmas with Frank Sinatra" and arranged by Gordon Jenkins.

The Christmas Waltz

Words by
SAMMY CAHN

Music by
JULE STYNE

Frank introduced this powerful song in the Academy Award winning short subject of the same name. He recorded it for Columbia on August 22, 1945.

The House I Live In

Words by
LEWIS ALLEN

Music by
EARL ROBINSON

This was one of Frank's earliest Columbia records. He also recorded it as part of the Capitol album "In The Wee Small Hours."

When Your Lover Has Gone

Words and Music by
E.A. SWAN

Frank's seventh recording as a solo artist (June 7, 1943), it was recorded with choir accompaniment during the AFM recording ban.

You'll Never Know

(From "Hello Frisco Hello")

Words by
MACK GORDON

Music by
HARRY WARREN

Moderato

Dar - ling, I'm so blue with - out you,__ I think a - bout you__ the live - long day.

When you ask me if I'm lone - ly,__ then I have on - ly this to say:

1. & 2. You'll nev - er know__ just how much_____ I miss you,

The third side recorded for Frank's Reprise label, it appeared on the album "Ring-A-Ding-Ding." Johnny Mandel arranged and conducted it for the December 19, 1960 session.

In The Still Of The Night

Words and Music by
COLE PORTER

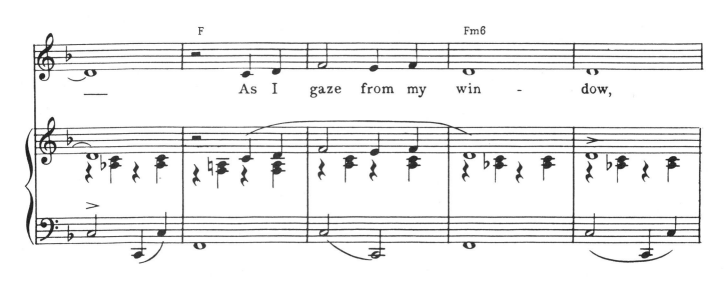

This unforgettable version of the Rodgers and Hart classic was taped on February 18, 1963 with a full symphony orchestra. The album was "The Concert Sinatra".

My Heart Stood Still

From "A Connecticut Yankee"

Words by
LORENZ HART

Music by
RICHARD RODGERS

From "Girl Crazy," Frank sang this for the recording microphone on December 19, 1944.

Embraceable You

Music and Lyrics by
GEORGE GERSHWIN and IRA GERSHWIN

Recorded on February 16, 1955, this song appears on Frank's "In The Wee Small Hours" album.

What Is This Thing Called Love?

Words and Music by
COLE PORTER

A Kurt Weill-Ogden Nash collaboration, this was a favorite on Frank's "Songs by Sinatra" radio program.

Speak Low

Words by
OGDEN NASH

Music by
KURT WEILL

For the film "High Society," Frank sang one of Cole Porter's last ballads. Two separate takes were made, one for the single (April 5, 1956) and for the soundtrack album (April 20, 1956).

You're Sensational

Words and Music by
COLE PORTER

"Sinatra Swings" was Frank's second Reprise album. It featured this song with a Billy May score recorded on May 18, 1961.

Love Walked In

Music and Lyrics by
GEORGE GERSHWIN and IRA GERSHWIN

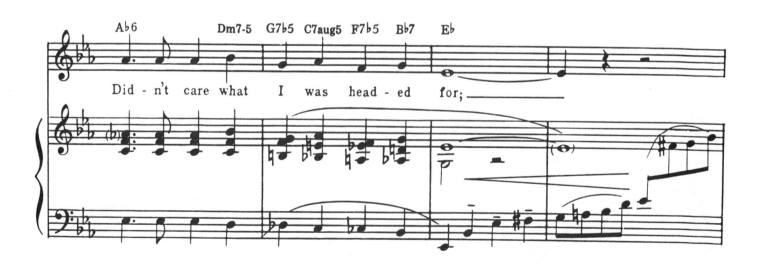

Refrain *(slowly, with much expression)*

Neal Hefti arranged this John Mercer classic for "Sinatra and Swingin' Brass." The recording took place on April 11, 1962.

Goody Goody

Words and Music by
JOHNNY MERCER and MATT MALNECK

One of the sides Frank made with Harry James and his orchestra. When first released in 1939, it caused nary a stir. But when Columbia re-released it during the war, the company could not press copies of it fast enough to satisfy the demand.

All Or Nothing At All

Words by
JACK LAWRENCE

Music by
ARTHUR ALTMAN

Billy May arranged this song for "Come Dance with Me." It was recorded on December 9, 1958.

Just In Time

(From "Bells Are Ringing")

Words by
BETTY COMDEN
and ADOLPH GREEN

Music by
JULE STYNE

Part of Frank's first recording session as a solo artist, he recorded it for RCA Bluebird on January 19, 1942. Axel
Stordahl penned the beautiful arrangement.

Night And Day

French Version by
EMÉLIA RENAUD

Words and Music by
COLE PORTER

Frank appeared with Jimmy Durante in the MGM film "It Happened in Brooklyn" and introduced this timeless Cahn-Styne song. He recorded it twice: for Columbia (October 24, 1946) and for Capitol (November 25, 1957).

From The Metro Goldwyn Mayer Picture "It Happened In Brooklyn"

Time After Time

Lyric by
SAMMY CAHN

Music by
JULE STYNE

Verse

What good are words I say to you? They can't con-vey to you what's in my heart. If you could hear in-stead The things I've left un-said! **Chorus** TIME AF-TER TIME I tell my-self that I'm So luck-y to be

One of the numerous Gershwin standards Frank has sung throughout the years.

They All Laughed

Music and Lyrics by
GEORGE GERSHWIN and IRA GERSHWIN

168

FILMWAYS
PICTURES
CONGRATULATES

FRANK
SINATRA

ON HIS
OUTSTANDING
PERFORMANCE
IN

THE
FIRST
DEADLY SIN

Young Blue Eyes

One of the most popular Sinatra recordings ever made. This was the main theme from the motion picture of the same name in which Frank starred with Doris Day.

Young At Heart

Words by
CAROLYN LEIGH

Music by
JOHNNY RICHARDS

Another song Frank continues to sing, it was part of "THE MAIN EVENT" concert at Madison Square Garden.
He'd recorded it twice before — for Columbia on December 4, 1947, and for Capitol (October 3, 1957).

Autumn In New York

Words and Music by
VERNON DUKE

Andantino *(poco rubato)*

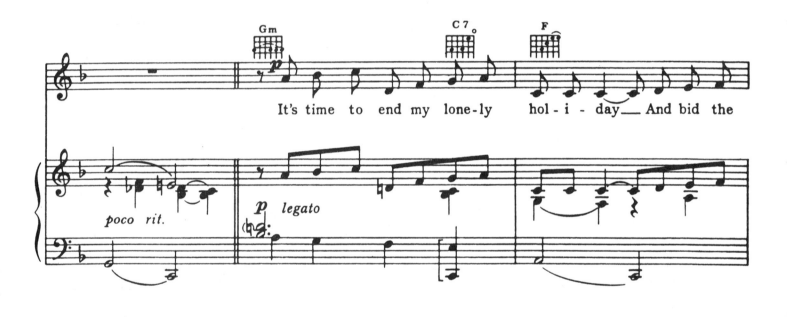

It's time to end my lone-ly hol-i-day __ And bid the

coun-try a has-ty fare - well. So on this gray and mel-an-

"Songs for Young Lovers" had this swinging George Siravo score which Frank recorded on November 5, 1953, his fourth recording session for Capitol.

A Foggy Day
(From "A Damsel In Distress")

Music and Lyrics by
GEORGE GERSHWIN and IRA GERSHWIN

Moderato

I was a strang-er in the cit-y.___ Out of town were the peo-ple I knew.

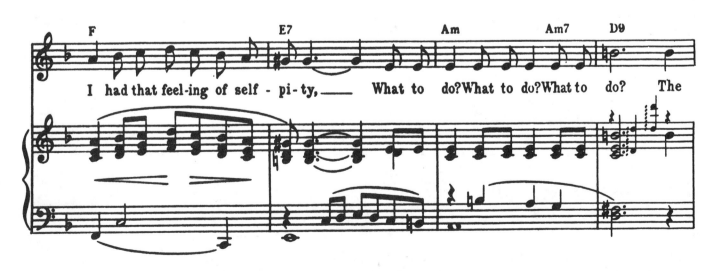

I had that feel-ing of self - pi-ty,___ What to do? What to do? What to do? The

out-look was de-cid-ed-ly blue.___ But as I walked through the fog-gy streets a-lone, It

turned out to be the luck-iest day I've known.___

Refrain *(brighter but warmly)*

A fog-gy day___ in Lon-don town___

Had me low___ and had me down.___

Gordon Jenkins wrote some of his finest arrangements for Frank's album "Where Are You." This song was transcribed on May 1, 1957.

I Cover The Waterfront

Words by
EDWARD HEYMAN

Music by
JOHN GREEN

Composed by Phil Silvers and Jimmy Van Heusen, this song has always been associated with Frank's first-born child, now a parent herself. It has become one of Frank's most popular Columbia sides.

Nancy
(With The Laughing Face)

Words by
PHIL SILVERS

Music by
JAMES VAN HEUSEN

Three unforgettable Sinatra versions circulate: Columbia (July 30, 1946 - Axel Stordahl arrangement), Capitol (September 11, 1961 - "Point of No Return" album), and Reprise (April 13, 1965 - a Gordon Jenkins score - "September of My Years.")

September Song

From "Knickerbocker Holiday"

Words by
MAXWELL ANDERSON

Music by
KURT WEILL

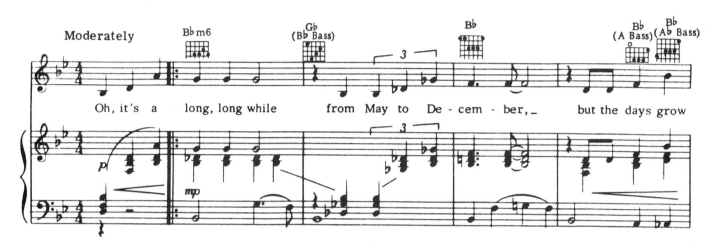

Oh, it's a long, long while from May to De-cem-ber,_ but the days grow

short, when you reach Sep-tem-ber._ When the au-tumn weath-er_

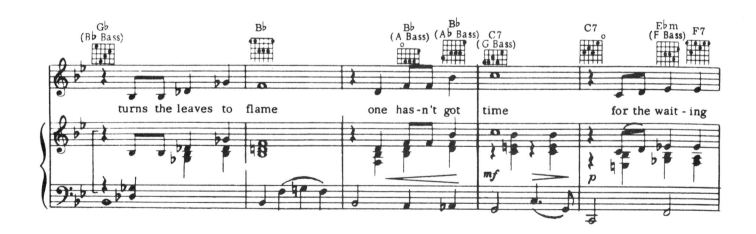

turns the leaves to flame one has-n't got time for the wait-ing

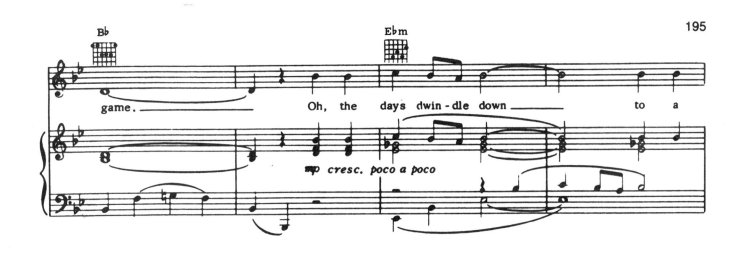

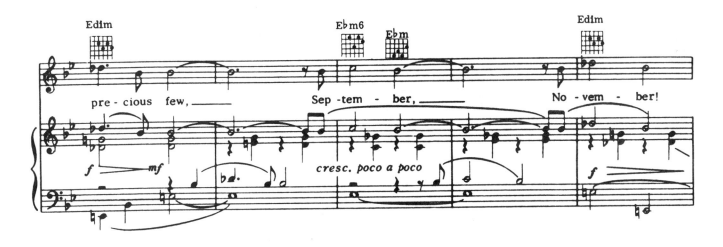

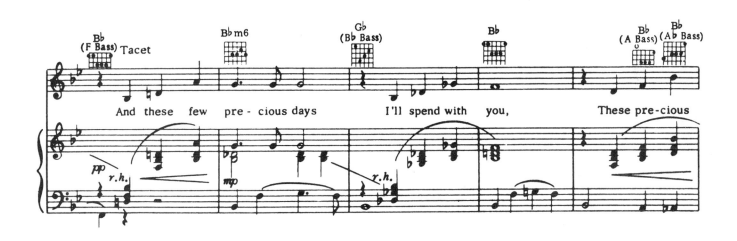

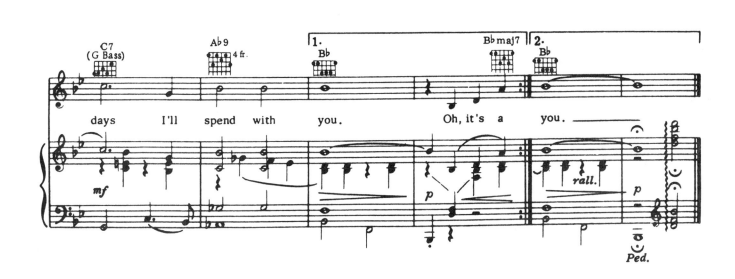

This Cahn-Styne song won an Academy Award. Sinatra taped it on March 1, 1954 with Nelson Riddle arranging and conducting. He redid it for Reprise on January 27, 1964 ("Sinatra's Sinatra" album).

Three Coins In The Fountain

Words by
SAMMY CAHN

Music by
JULE STYNE

Both Axel Stordahl and Nelson Riddle arranged this song. The former score was recorded on July 30, 1945; the latter, for the album "Nice And Easy", on March 1, 1960.

You Go To My Head

Words by
HAVEN GILLESPIE

Music by
J. FRED COOTS

Another classic from an early Capitol recording session (November 5, 1953), the score was by Nelson Riddle.

My Funny Valentine

Words by
LORENZ HART

Music by
RICHARD RODGERS

Be -hold the way our fine-feath-ered friend his vir - tue doth pa - rade. Thou

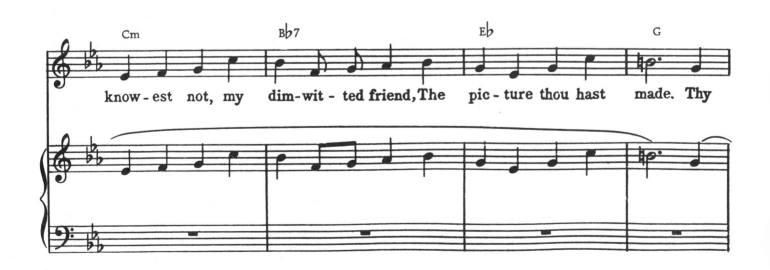

know- est not, my dim-wit - ted friend, The pic - ture thou hast made. Thy

Frank won an Academy Award for his portrayal of Maggio in the film of the same name. His recording of this song took place on May 2, 1953, his third session for Capitol and his second with Nelson Riddle arranging and conducting.

From Here To Eternity

Words by
ROBERT WELLS

Music by
FRED KARGER

From "A Hole in The Head," Frank recorded this beautiful Cahn-Van Heusen song with Nelson Riddle on December 29, 1958.

All My Tomorrows

Words by
SAMMY CAHN

Music by
JAMES VAN HEUSEN

Rodgers and Hammerstein masterpiece opened "The Concert Sinatra." Nelson Riddle arranged the song and ...ık recorded it at Samuel Goldwyn studios on February 19, 1963.

I Have Dreamed

(From "The King & I")

Words by
OSCAR HAMMERSTEIN II

Music by
RICHARD RODGERS

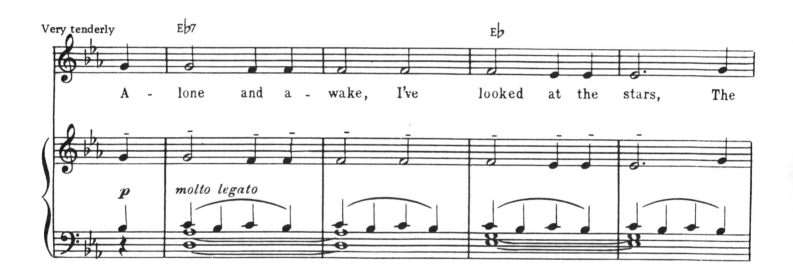

A - lone and a - wake, I've looked at the stars, The

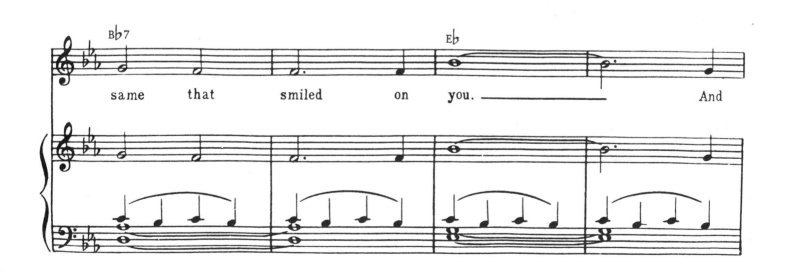

same that smiled on you. _____ And

I have dreamed _____ ev-'ry word you'll whis - per _____

When you're close, _____ close to me. _____

How you look _____ in the glow of eve - ning _____

I have dreamed _____ and en - joyed the

Frank first recorded this for Capitol on September 13, 1955 with Nelson Riddle's pen and baton. He later chose it for the Reprise album "Sinatra-Basie" with a score by Neal Hefti (recorded October 3, 1962).

(Love Is)
The Tender Trap

(From the film "The Tender Trap")

Words by
SAMMY CAHN

Music by
JAMES VAN HEUSEN

You see a pair of laugh-ing eyes_____ And
hand in hand be-neath the trees_____ And

sud-den-ly you're sigh-ing sighs,_____ You're
soon there's mu-sic in the breeze,_____ You're

hur - ry to a spot, that's just____ a dot on the map!

You won - der how____ it all____ came a - bout, It's too

__ late now,__ there's no____ get - ting out, You fell____ in love,__ and love____

__ is THE TEN-DER TRAP! _____

First sung in "Robin and The Seven Hoods," this is another often-requested song that Frank still performs in concert.

My Kind Of Town
(Chicago Is)

Words by
SAMMY CAHN

Music by
JAMES VAN HEUSEN

Don't ev-er, ev-er ask me what Chi-ca-go is, ___ Un-less you've got an hour or two or three. ___ 'Cause I need time to tell you what Chi-ca-go is, ___

CHORUS (nice walking style)

*) Any city name of three syllables can replace Chicago; such as Manhattan, Las Vegas, etc.

Recorded for "Songs for Swingin' Lovers" on January 16, 1956 with Nelson Riddle on the podium.

Too Marvelous For Words

Words by
JOHNNY MERCER

Music by
RICHARD A. WHITING

Most fans know this song with a Billy May arrangement. Recently, however, two separate recordings, one with a
Nelson Riddle score, the other with an Axel Stordahl arrangement, have been retrieved from the Capitol vaults.

Day In - Day Out

Words by
JOHNNY MERCER

Music by
RUBE BLOOM

Frank recorded this with Nelson Riddle on November 20, 1956 for "A Swingin' Affair" and also with "Swingin' Brass" on April 11, 1962 (Neal Hefti arranging and conducting).

At Long Last Love

Words and Music by
COLE PORTER

love,___ I've no sense of val - ues___ left at all.___ Is this a

play - time___ af-faire of May - time, Or is it a wind - fall?___

Refrain
slowly, with warm expression

Is it an earth quake ___ or sim - ply a shock?___

___ Is it the good tur - tle soup or mere - ly the

A wartime favorite, this was Frank's fifth side with the Tommy Dorsey Orchestra. He later re-recorded it for his own Reprise label with a new Sy Oliver score on May 1, 1961.

I'll Be Seeing You

Words and Music by
IRVING KAHAL and SAMMY FAIN

The "Songs for Swingin' Lovers" album included this, one of George Gershwin's last songs.

Love Is Here To Stay

Music and Lyrics by
GEORGE GERSHWIN and IRA GERSHWIN

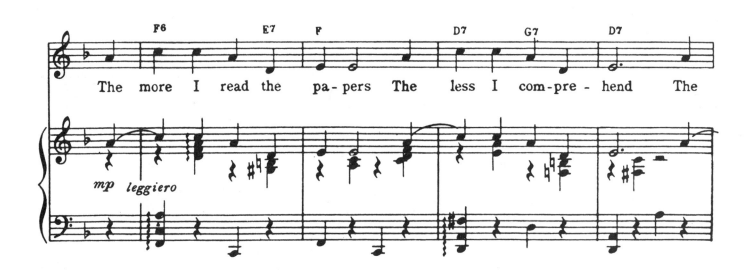

The more I read the pa-pers The less I com-pre-hend The

world and all its ca-pers And how it all will end. Noth-ing seems to be

The Sinatra fan has three versions of this showstopper. Two were recorded for Columbia (April 7 and May 28, 1946 - the latter is the rarer of the two) with an Axel Stordahl setting. The third was made for "The Concert Sinatra" album for Reprise.

Soliloquy

Lyrics by
OSCAR HAMMERSTEIN II

Music by
RICHARD RODGERS

246

"Our Town" was turned into a TV play with songs in 1955. Frank starred in the production and introduced this song which he recorded for Capitol on August 15, 1955.

Love And Marriage

Words by
SAMMY CAHN

Music by
JAMES VAN HEUSEN

The album "In The Wee Small Hours" was a treasure trove of great standards, including this bittersweet lament, arranged by Nelson Riddle and recorded on February 8, 1955.

Glad To Be Unhappy

Words by
LORENZ HART

Music by
RICHARD RODGERS

Look at your-self; If you had a sense of hu-mor, you would laugh to beat the Band.

Look at your-self; Do you still be-lieve the ru-mor that ro-

Frank's two recordings are both gems: the first had an Axel Stordahl score (recorded on October 9, 1950); the second had a rockin' Billy May arrangement for the "Come Fly With Me" album (October 3, 1957).

April In Paris

"Avril à Paris"

Words by
E.Y. HARBURG
French Version by
EMELIA RENAUD

Music by
VERNON DUKE

Axel Stordahl collaborated with noted arranger Paul Weston and Sammy Cahn, and the same team that wrote DAY BY DAY came up with another standard. Stordahl arranged this song for Frank's recording session of March 6, 1945.

I Should Care

Words and Music by
SAMMY CAHN, AXEL STORDAHL
and PAUL WESTON

From the show "On Your Toes," Sinatra sang this song in the musical film "Pal Joey" with a Nelson Riddle score.

There's A Small Hotel

(From "On Your Toes")

Words by
LORENZ HART

Music by
RICHARD RODGERS

She: I'd like to get a-way, Jun-ior, Some-where a-lone with you.

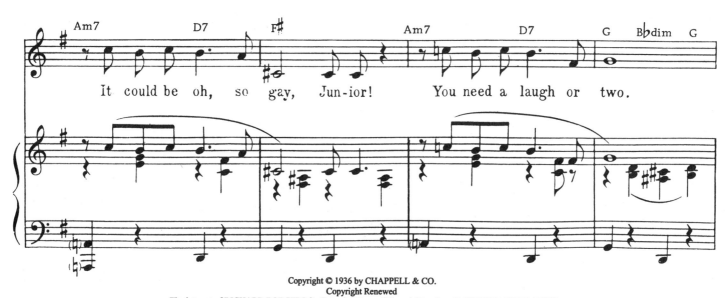

It could be oh, so gay, Jun-ior! You need a laugh or two.

There's a brid-al suite; One room bright and neat, Com-

plete for us to share to-geth - er.

Look-ing through the win - dow you can see a dis-tant stee-ple;

Not a sign of peo-ple, Who wants peo-ple?

Another huge hit for Sinatra and Capitol! Cy Coleman and Carolyn Leigh collaborated on the song, and Nelson Riddle wrote the arrangement. Sinatra re-recorded it for Reprise ("Sinatra's Sinatra") on April 30, 1963.

Witchcraft

Words by
CAROLYN LEIGH

Music by
CY COLEMAN

Part of the album "Songs for Swingin' Lovers," recorded with Nelson Riddle conducting on January 6, 1956.

I Thought About You

Words by
JOHNNY MERCER

Music by
JIMMY VAN HEUSEN

Seems that I read, — or some-bod-y said — That out of sight is out of mind, — May-be that's so — but I tried to go — And leave you be-hind, — What did I find? —

First taped for the soundtrack of "Can-Can" on February 19, 1960, Frank recorded a swinging Sammy Nestico score for the "L.A. Is My Lady" album.

It's All Right With Me

Words and Music by
COLE PORTER

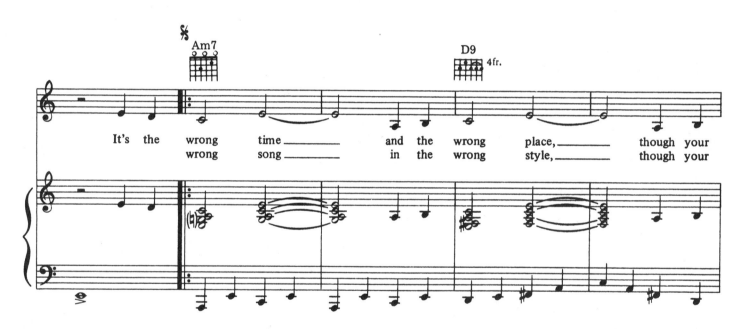

It's the wrong time _____ and the wrong place, _____ though your
wrong song _____ in the wrong style, _____ though your

face is charm - ing it's the wrong face. _____ It's not
smile is love - ly it's the wrong smile. _____ It's not

D. S. 𝄋 *(with repeats) al Coda* ⊕

C6   E7   E7   F7

Coda

me. _____ *Inst.* _____   too.

B♭m7   E♭9

Wrong game _____ with the wrong chips, _____ Though your

B♭m7   E♭m7

lips are tempt - ing they're the wrong lips. _____ They're not

A♭7   F7-5   B♭9

her chops _____ but they're such tempt - ing chops _____ that if

Written for the motion picture starring Debbie Reynolds, this was Reprise's first 45 single. Frank recorded it with
Felix Slatkin at the podium on December 21, 1960.

The Second Time Around

Words and Music by
SAMMY CAHN
and JAMES VAN HEUSEN

Love is love-li-er THE SEC-OND TIME A-ROUND, Just as won-der-ful with both feet on the ground. It's that sec-ond time you hear your love song sung,

Part of the classic "Only The Lonely" album, this was taped on June 24, 1958, with Nelson Riddle arranging and conducting.

What's New?

Words by
JOHNNY BURKE

Music by
BOB HAGGART

289

George Siravo's arrangement helped make this one of Frank's swingingest Columbia sides on April 14, 1950.

You Do Something To Me

Words and Music by
COLE PORTER

Some-thing that sim-ply mys-ti - fies me.

Tell me, why should it be

You have the pow'r to hyp-no - tize me?

Let me live 'neath your spell,

Billy Butterfield soloed on Frank's Columbia version of October 9, 1950. Frank recorded the song for Capitol on March 2, 1960 for the "Nice and Easy" album.

Nevertheless

(I'm In Love With You)

Words and Music by
BERT KALMAR and HARRY RUBY

I knew the time had to come, When I'd be held un-der your
In spite of all I could do, I went a-head fall-ing for

thumb.   I'm like a pawn in your hand, Moved and com-
you.   So if I laugh or I cry, I made my

Fine at the start, then left with a heart that is break - ing.

May-be I'll live _ a life of re-gret_ And may-be I'll give_ much

more than I'll get;_ But, Nev-er-the-less,_ I'm In Love With

1.

2.

You. _____

You. _____

Both Sinatra recordings are classics. The first was recorded with an Axel Stordahl score. The second, for "Only The Lonely," was recorded on May 29, 1958 with a Nelson Riddle arrangement.

Guess I'll Hang My Tears Out To Dry

Words by
SAMMY CAHN

Music by
JULE STYNE

Don Costa's first album with Sinatra was "Sinatra and Strings," and this song ended side one. It was taped on November 22, 1961.

Come Rain Or Come Shine

Words by
JOHNNY MERCER

Music by
HAROLD ARLEN

Written for the film "Papa's Delicate Condition," Frank's version appeared on the Reprise album "Sinatra's Sinatra" with an arrangement by Nelson Riddle.

Call Me Irresponsible

Words by
SAMMY CAHN

Music by
JAMES VAN HEUSEN

Slowly

Verse, with a trace of self-pity

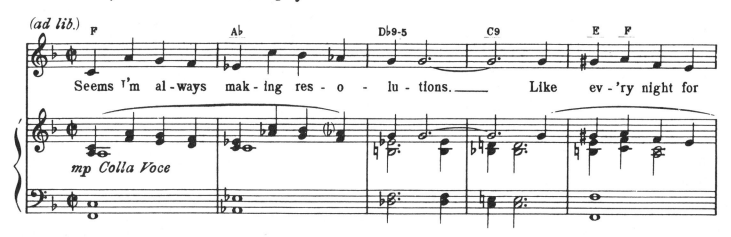

Refrain, Slowly With A Smooth, Steady Rhythm

Frank's rendition was a highlight of the MGM musical "Anchors Aweigh." His Columbia recording took place on December 1, 1944.

I Fall In Love Too Easily

Words and Music by
SAMMY CAHN and JULE STYNE

Sinatra had Quincy Jones score this for his appearance at the Sands Hotel with Count Basie. It appeared on "Sinatra at The Sands."

Where Or When

(From "Babes In Arms")

Words by
LORENZ HART

Music by
RICHARD RODGERS

Another song Frank recorded twice, Columbia recorded it on November 5, 1947 with Axel Stordahl supplying the arrangement. Later, Nelson Riddle scored it for the album "In the Wee Small Hours."

It Never Entered My Mind

Words by
LORENZ HART

Music by
RICHARD RODGERS

Arlen and Mercer wrote one of the definitive "saloon" songs for the film "The Sky's The Limit." Frank has recorded it three times.

One For My Baby
(And One More For The Road)

Words by
JOHNNY MERCER

Music by
HAROLD ARLEN

The classic Columbia Sinatra-Stordahl recording was made on March 6, 1945. Frank later re-recorded the song, this time with Nelson Riddle arranging, for "Nice 'n Easy."

Dream

Words and Music by
JOHNNY MERCER

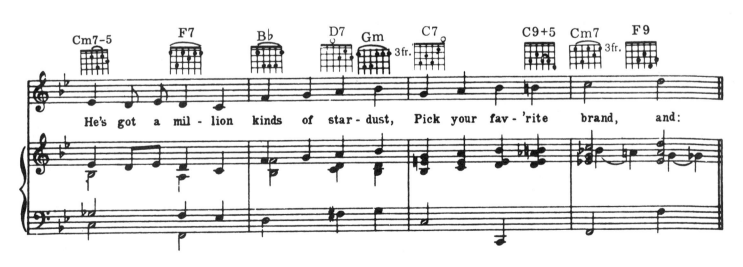

CHORUS *(Slow tempo)*

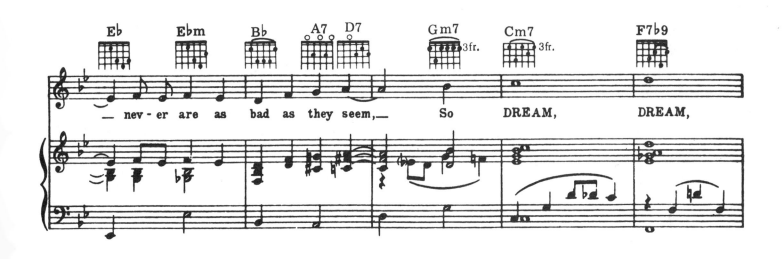

A classic song, with a now-classic Nelson Riddle arrangement, recorded on April 7, 1954.

Just One Of Those Things

Words and Music by
COLE PORTER

Frank turned this Gershwin song into a standard with his recording, made with Axel Stordahl on November 5, 1947. The recording featured a solo by trumpeter Bobby Hackett.

I've Got A Crush On You

Music and Lyrics by
GEORGE GERSHWIN and IRA GERSHWIN

Another song Frank liked enough to record twice: once for Capitol (arranger, Nelson Riddle; November 20, 1956)
and for Reprise (Count Basie orchestra-arranger: Neal Hefti; October 2, 1962).

Nice Work If You Can Get It

(From "A Damsel In Distress")

Music and Lyrics by
GEORGE GERSHWIN and IRA GERSHWIN

The man who on-ly lives for mak-ing mon-ey Lives a life that is-n't nec-es-sa-ri-ly sun-ny. Like-wise the man who works for fame,

Refrain: *(smoothly)*

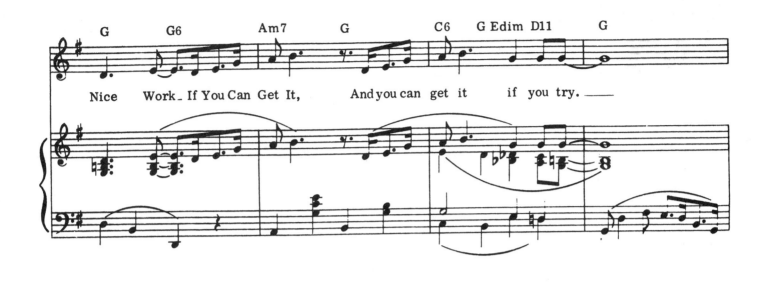

Nice Work. If You Can Get It, And you can get it if you try. ___

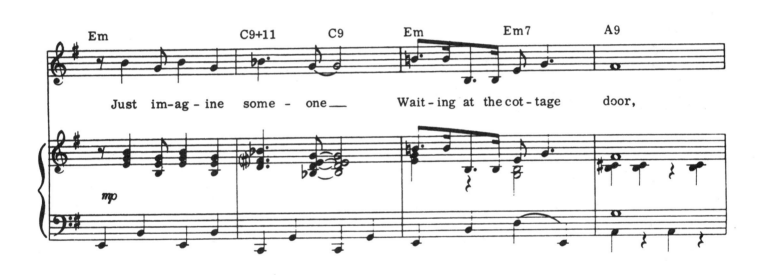

Just im-ag-ine some-one___ Wait-ing at the cot-tage door,

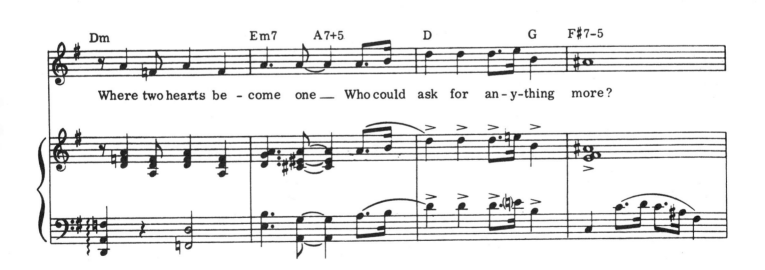

Where two hearts be-come one ___ Who could ask for an-y-thing more?

Frank taped this song, one of his biggest hits, on May 16, 1966. His recording was featured prominently in the
film "The Pope of Greenwich Village."

Summer Wind

English Words by
JOHNNY MERCER

Music by
HENRY MAYER

The SUM-MER WIND came blow-ing in a-cross the sea,— It
lin-gered there to touch your hair and walk with me.— All
sum-mer long we sang a song and strolled the gold-en sand,

Another instant standard, the recording was made on May 8, 1959 with Nelson Riddle's arrangement and "A Bunch of Kids."

High Hopes

Words by
SAMMY CAHN

Music by
JAMES VAN HEUSEN

Moderato (with a beat)

1. Next time you're found with your chin on the ground, There's a
2. When trou-bles call and your back's to the wall, There's a

lot to be learned, So look a - round.
lot to be learned, That wall could fall.

Refrain

Just what makes that lit-tle ol' ant Think he'll move that
Once there was a sil-ly ol' ram, Thought he'd punch a

Another often-requested Sinatra song, Billy May was responsible for the unforgettable arrangement first recorded on October 8, 1957. Frank re-recorded it for Reprise on October 11, 1965 for the album "Sinatra: A Man and His Music."

Come Fly With Me

Words by
SAMMY CAHN

Music by
JAMES VAN HEUSEN

Recorded for the soundtrack of the movie "Pal Joey" on August 13, 1957 (Nelson Riddle arranged).

I Could Write A Book

(From "Pal Joey")

Words by
LORENZ HART

Music by
RICHARD RODGERS

From the "In The Wee Small Hours" album, this Nelson Riddle score was cut on February 8, 1955.

Dancing On The Ceiling

(He Dances On My Ceiling)

Words by
LORENZ HART

Music by
RICHARD RODGERS

This was one of the last records Frank recorded for Columbia on June 3, 1952. Axel Stordahl provided the orchestration.

The Birth Of The Blues

Words by
B.G. DeSYLVA and LEW BROWN

Music by
RAY HENDERSON

Dietz and Schwartz wrote this classic in 1937 for the show "Between the Devil." Frank recorded it with Nelson
Riddle on February 16, 1955 for the album "In the Wee Small Hours."

I See Your Face Before Me

Words by
HOWARD DIETZ

Music by
ARTHUR SCHWARTZ

FRANK SINATRA FILMOGRAPHY

1941
LAS VEGAS NIGHTS
Paramount

1943
SHIP AHOY
MGM

1943
REVEILLE WITH BEVERLY
Columbia

1943
HIGHER AND HIGHER
RKO

1944
STEP LIVELY
RKO

1945
ANCHORS AWEIGH
MGM

1945
THE HOUSE I LIVE IN
RKO

1946
TILL THE CLOUDS ROLL BY
MGM

1947
IT HAPPENED IN BROOKLYN
MGM

1948
THE MIRACLE OF THE BELLS
RKO

1948
THE KISSING BANDIT
MGM

1949
TAKE ME OUT TO THE BALLGAME
MGM

1949
ON THE TOWN
MGM

1951
MEET DANNY WILSON
Universal-International

1951
DOUBLE DYNAMITE
RKO

1953
FROM HERE TO ETERNITY
Columbia

1954
SUDDENLY
United Artists

1955
YOUNG AT HEART
Warner Bros.

1955
NOT AS A STRANGER
United Artists

1955
THE TENDER TRAP
MGM

1955
GUYS AND DOLLS
MGM

1955
THE MAN WITH THE GOLDEN ARM
United Artists

1956
MEET ME IN LAS VEGAS
MGM

1956
HIGH SOCIETY
MGM

1956
JOHNNY CONCHO
United Artists

1956
AROUND THE WORLD IN 80 DAYS
United Artists

1957
THE PRIDE AND THE PASSION
United Artists

1957
THE JOKER IS WILD
Paramount

1957
PAL JOEY
Columbia

1958
KINGS GO FORTH
United Artists

1958
SOME CAME RUNNING
MGM

1959
A HOLE IN THE HEAD
United Artists

1959
NEVER SO FEW
MGM

1960
CAN-CAN
Twentieth Century-Fox

1960
OCEAN'S ELEVEN
Warner Bros.

1960
PEPE
Columbia

1961
THE DEVIL AT 4 O'CLOCK
Columbia

1962
SERGEANT'S THREE
United Artists

1962
THE ROAD TO HONG KONG
United Artists

1962
THE MANCHURIAN CANDIDATE
United Artists

1963
THE LIST OF ADRIAN MESSENGE
Universal

1963
COME BLOW YOUR HORN
Paramount

1964
FOUR FOR TEXAS
Warner Bros.

1964
ROBIN AND THE SEVEN HOODS
Warner Bros.

1965
NONE BUT THE BRAVE
Warner Bros.

1965
VON RYAN'S EXPRESS
Twentieth Century-Fox

1965
MARRIAGE ON THE ROCKS
Warner Bros.

1966
THE OSCAR
Embassy Pictures

1966
CAST A GIANT SHADOW
United Artists

1966
ASSAULT ON A QUEEN
Paramount

1967
THE NAKED RUNNER
Warner Bros.

FRANK SINATRA FILMOGRAPHY, CONT'D

1967
TONY ROME
Twentieth Century-Fox

1968
THE DETECTIVE
Twentieth Century-Fox

1968
LADY IN CEMENT
Twentieth Century-Fox

1970
DIRTY DINGUS MAGEE
MGM

1974
THAT'S ENTERTAINMENT
MGM

1976
THAT'S ENTERTAINMENT PART II
MGM

1980
FIRST DEADLY SIN
Filmways

1984
CANNONBALL RUN II
Golden Harvest Films

FRANK SINATRA – THE ALBUMS

FABULOUS FRANKIE
THE VOICE OF FRANK SINATRA
CHRISTMAS SONGS BY SINATRA
FRANK SINATRA - FRANKLY SENTIMENTAL
SONGS BY SINATRA - VOL. 1
FRANK SINATRA - DEDICATED TO YOU
SING AND DANCE WITH FRANK SINATRA
I'VE GOT A CRUSH ON YOU FRANK SINATRA
DORIS DAY/FRANK SINATRA -
   YOUNG AT HEART
GET HAPPY (HOUSE PARTY SERIES)
I'VE GOT A CRUSH ON YOU
   (HOUSE PARTY SERIES)
CHRISTMAS WITH SINATRA
   (HOUSE PARTY SERIES)
FRANK SINATRA - SONGS FOR YOUNG LOVERS
SWING EASY!
FRANK SINATRA . . . WEE SMALL HOURS
THE VOICE
FRANK SINATRA CONDUCTS THE MUSIC OF
   ALEX WILDER
FRANK SINATRA - SONGS FOR
   SWINGIN' LOVERS
FRANK SINATRA - THAT OLD FEELING
FRANK SINATRA - ADVENTURES OF
   THE HEART
FRANK SINATRA CONDUCTS TONE POEMS
   OF COLOR
FRANKIE
HIGH SOCIETY
THIS IS SINATRA!
FRANK SINATRA - CLOSE TO YOU
FRANK SINATRA - A SWINGIN' AFFAIR!
FRANK SINATRA - CHRISTMAS DREAMING
A JOLLY CHRISTMAS FROM FRANK SINATRA
PAL JOEY
FRANKIE AND TOMMY
WHERE ARE YOU? - FRANK SINATRA
WE 3 - FRANK SINATRA,
   TOMMY DORSEY, AXEL STORDAHL
THE MAN I LOVE - PEGGY LEE,
   FRANK SINATRA

COME FLY WITH ME - FRANK SINATRA
FRANK SINATRA - PUT YOUR DREAMS AWAY
THIS IS SINATRA - VOLUME TWO
FRANK SINATRA SINGS FOR ONLY THE LONELY
FRANK SINATRA - COME DANCE WITH ME!
THE FRANK SINATRA STORY IN MUSIC
POINT OF NO RETURN - FRANK SINATRA
SINATRA AND SWINGIN' BRASS
SINATRA SINGS GREAT SONGS FROM
   GREAT BRITAIN
FRANK SINATRA CONDUCTS MUSIC FROM
   PICTURES AND PLAYS
THE CONCERT SINATRA
TOMMY DORSEY AND HIS ORCHESTRA
   FEATURING FRANK SINATRA
SINATRA-BASIE - AN HISTORIC MUSICAL
   FIRST
SINATRA SINGS . . . OF LOVE AND THINGS
FRANK SINATRA - ALL ALONE
SOUTH PACIFIC
KISS ME KATE
GUYS AND DOLLS
FINIAN'S RAINBOW
SINATRA'S SINATRA
FRANK SINATRA - HAVE YOURSELF A MERRY
   LITTLE CHRISTMAS
DAYS OF WINE AND ROSES - MOON RIVER AND
   OTHER ACADEMY AWARD WINNERS
AMERICAN I HEAR YOU SINGING -
   FRANK SINATRA, BING CROSBY,
   FRED WARING
IT MIGHT AS WELL BE SWING
ROBIN AND THE 7 HOODS
FRANK SINATRA SINGS RODGERS AND HART
SOFTLY, AS I LEAVE YOU - SINATRA
BING CROSBY, FRANK SINATRA,
   FRED WARING - 12 SONGS OF CHRISTMAS
FRANK SINATRA - SEPTEMBER OF MY YEARS
SINATRA '65
TELL HER YOU LOVE HER - FRANK SINATRA
FRANK SINATRA - MY KIND OF BROADWAY
FRANK SINATRA - A MAN AND HIS MUSIC

FRANK SINATRA — THE ALBUMS, CONT'D

FRANK SINATRA - STRANGERS IN THE NIGHT
MOONLIGHT SINATRA
SINATRA AT THE SANDS WITH COUNT BASIE
    AND THE ORCHESTRA
FOREVER FRANK
FRANK SINATRA - THAT'S LIFE
FRANCIS ALBERT SINATRA &
    ANTONIO CARLOS JOBIM
THE ESSENTIAL FRANK SINATRA
FRANK SINATRA - AND FRANK 7 NANCY -
    SOMETHIN STUPID
FRANK SINATRA - IN HOLLYWOOD 1943-1949
SLEEP WARM - DEAN MARTIN WITH
    ORCHESTRA CONDUCTED BY
    FRANK SINATRA
FRANK SINATRA - LOOK TO YOUR HEART
NO ONE CARES - FRANK SINATRA
CAN - CAN
SWING EASY!
NICE -N- EASY
THE BROADWAY KICK - FRANK SINATRA
FRANK SINATRA - COME BACK TO SORRENTO
FRANK SINATRA - LOVE IS A KICK
FRANK SINATRA - SONGS FOR YOUNG LOVERS
SINATRA'S SWING' SESSION!!!
RING-A-DING DING!
REFLECTIONS - FRANK SINATRA
FRANK SINATRA - ALL THE WAY
SINATRA SWINGS
FRANK SINATRA - COME SWING WITH ME!
I REMEMBER TOMMY - FRANK SINATRA

SINATRA & STRINGS
FRANCIS A. & EDWARD K.
FRANK SINATRA'S GREATEST HITS!
FRANK SINATRA - CYCLES
THE SINATRA FAMILY WISH YOU A
    MERRY CHRISTMAS
MY WAY - FRANK SINATRA
FRANK SINATRA - A MAN ALONE
FRANK SINATRA
SINATRA & COMPANY
FRANK SINATRA'S GREATEST HITS VOL. 2
THIS LOVE OF MINE - FRANK SINATRA WITH
    THE TOMMY DORSEY ORCHESTRA
OL' BLUE EYES IS BACK
FRANK SINATRA
SINATRA - THE MAIN EVENT LIVE
SINATRA - TRILOGY
SINATRA - SHE SHOT ME DOWN
THE TOMMY DORSEY, FRANK SINATRA
    SESSIONS - VOL. 1
THE TOMMY DORSEY, FRANK SINATRA
    SESSIONS - VOL. 2
THE TOMMY DORSEY, FRANK SINATRA
    SESSIONS - VOL. 3
SYMS BY SINATRA
THE TOMMY DORSEY, FRANK SINATRA
    RADIO YEARS 1940-42 AND THE HISTORIC
    STORDAHL SESSION
FRANK SINATRA - L.A. IS MY LADY WITH
    QUINCY JONES AND ORCHESTRA
FRANK SINATRA - THE VOICE/THE COLUMBIA
    YEARS 1943-1952